CHILDREN'S STORIES ABOUT CHESSED

BY MENUCHA FUCHS

Illustrations by Yoni

Translated by Zelda Goldfield

Adapted by B. Goldman

The Judaica Press, Inc. ◆ New York ◆ 1999

ISBN 1-880582-44-9

THE JUDAICA PRESS, INC.
718-972-6200   800-972-6201
info@judaicapress.com
www.judaicapress.com

Manufactured in the United States of America

TABLE OF CONTENTS

WHAT IS A GEMACH?

The word gemach comes from the Hebrew *gemilus chasadim*, which means acting towards others in a kind way. Jews all over the world have started gemachs to help friends and neighbors. There are gemachs for brides who need a beautiful wedding dress—or for anybody who might need clothes for a special occasion. There are also gemachs to help people in their day-to-day lives. Setting up a gemach is just one more way in which Jews are able to help one another.

MEET THE COHEN FAMILY

Ruti: It's not easy being the oldest of ten children, but if anyone can do it, eighteen-year-old Ruti can!

Zisi: Fifteen-year-old Zisi always goes out of her way to help anyone—whether they are a member of her family, a friend or a stranger.

Mordechai: Twelve-year-old Mordechai is the oldest of the Cohen boys. Though not yet bar mitzvah, Mordechai takes his responsibilities very seriously and thinks of himself as Abba's main helper.

Rina: Eleven-year-old Rina would like to keep up with her older sisters and often plans to do "grown up" things with Zisi. She also loves talking to and playing with her friends.

Efrayim: Nine-year-old Efrayim is known as "Efrayim Mishkafayim" because of the glasses he must always wear.

Eliezer: Curious and mischievous, seven-year-old Eliezer enjoys experimenting and exploring his world.

Miri: Adorable Miri is three-years-old. She always makes sure her brothers and sisters know she is there—even when they try to ignore her!

Naftali: Though only two-years-old, Naftali already thinks of himself as a "big boy."

Penina: One-year-old Penina is the youngest girl in the Cohen family.

...And the newest member of the family: **another little brother**!

CHAPTER ONE

A MEDICINE GEMACH

It was Friday night. The candles were still burning as we sat in the dining room and Abba told us stories about great rabbis from long ago. Penina, my one-year-old baby sister, sat on Ima's lap and laughed.

I love being with my family on Friday

1

nights. It's so quiet and everyone is always so happy during these times. We study with Abba and little Penina just laughs and laughs.

Just like clock work, every Friday night, two-year-old Naftali falls asleep at the table. Ima carries him to his room and helps him put on his pajamas. Miri follows them and goes to bed, too. Abba continues to tell us stories. When he sees my eyes closing he says: "Mordechai, go to bed." I run into my bed, cover myself with my blanket, say *Shema Yisrael,* and fall asleep.

This Friday night was different. As I pulled the blanket over my head, I heard loud cries. At first I thought there was a cat in our yard. But when Ima began to rock Penina's bed, I knew it was Penina who was crying. Ima took Penina's temperature. It was very high and Ima was worried. When she gave Penina her medicine, Penina licked the spoon and stopped crying. Soon the room was quiet and I fell asleep.

Later that night, Penina began to cry again. I got up and looked outside. It was still dark. The Shabbos candles had burned out and I couldn't see anything. I heard Abba and Ima talking. I knew they were worried, so I got out of bed and went to the living room.

The street lamp lit up the room. Ima was sitting on the sofa and holding Penina. Abba was standing near the window. When Penina saw me she tried to smile. But she soon began to cry again. She picked up her hand and put it on her ear.

"I think her ear hurts," Ima said.

Ima asked me to hold Penina and went to look for more medicine. She came back with an empty bottle of ear drops.

"What should we do?" she asked.

"I have an idea," I said. "I'll go to Rabbi Pollack's house. He has a medicine gemach. He doesn't live far away. But do you think we can knock on his door now? It's very late."

"We have no choice," Ima said sadly.

"What's wrong with Penina?" I asked.

"She's sick and the medicine didn't help," Abba said. "She can't sleep."

I got dressed quickly, and Abba and I hurried to Rabbi Pollack's house. The streets were completely empty. The houses were all dark. Only the street lamps shone.

We reached Rabbi Pollack's house. The street lamp was near his door and we saw his name on the mailbox. Near the mailbox was a small sign that said:

<u>MEDICINE GEMACH</u>

Open:
24 hours a day

Refuah Shlaima

"Did you see that sign?" Abba asked in surprise.

"Yes!" I answered happily.

We hurried up the stairs, and knocked on Rabbi Pollack's door.

We knocked quietly, because we thought the Pollacks would be sleeping. No one answered. We knocked a second time, then a third. At last someone asked: "Who's there?"

"I'm sorry for coming so late. But my baby's running a high fever," Abba said.

The door opened. Rabbi Pollack was wearing a robe.

"Can I help you?" he asked.

"I need ear drops for my baby daughter. I'm sorry we woke you," Abba apologized.

"Don't worry," Rabbi Pollack replied. "It's a mitzvah to help people. Please come in."

Rabbi Pollack went inside and came back out with a small bottle of ear drops.

"Here, this should help you. I hope

your daughter feels better soon!" He wished us a good Shabbos and waved good-bye.

Abba and I walked home silently. Ima met us at the door, took the bottle, and gave Penina some ear drops. Then we all went to bed.

The next morning my head hurt a little. But I got out of bed because I didn't want to be late for *Shacharis*. When I passed by Rabbi Pollack's house, I ran over to the mailbox and read the small sign over and over again. A wonderful feeling filled my heart.

"Jews are so kind! They have such good hearts, and want to help others even in the middle of the night on Shabbos. Who knows what would have happened to Penina without this medicine! I'm so proud to be a Jew!" I thought.

Gemach for
Lost Children

CHAPTER TWO

LOST CHILDREN

"Can I take Naftali with me?" I asked Ima.

"Where are you going?" she asked.

"To Avigdor's house," I answered. "Naftali can come along. Avigdor's little brothers will play with him. There is a small slide in the park near his house, and some sand, too."

"Fine," Ima said. "I have to go shopping and will come back in about an hour. Ruti can stay home with the little ones."

Ima left. I took Naftali's hand and went to Avigdor's house.

Many children were playing in the park.

"Do you want to play with them?" I asked Naftali.

Naftali didn't answer. Instead he ran over to the sandbox.

"Do you want to go inside?" Avigdor asked me. "It's very noisy in the park."

We went inside and sat down on the sofa.

"Do you want to play with my puzzle?"

"Sure," I replied.

We played for nearly an hour. Suddenly I remembered Naftali.

"Oh, no!" I cried. "I left my brother in the park!"

"Don't worry. There are lots of kids in

the park," Avigdor said.

But I was very worried. I went to the park, but I didn't see Naftali.

"Where is he?" I asked the other children.

"He went outside," one kid said.

"Outside?" I shouted. "Where?"

"We don't know," they said shaking their heads.

At that moment, a woman passed by and stopped in front of the sandbox. "Excuse me," she said. Do you know a little boy who is wearing a yellow shirt and green pants?"

"He's my brother!" I shouted, so excited I jumped up and down. "Where is he?"

The woman pointed to the house next door to the park.

I quickly ran there and saw Naftali. He was standing near a sign that said: *"Gemach for Lost Children."*

"Is this your brother?" a nice lady standing near the sign asked. "Someone found him on the street and brought him here. We sent helpers all over the neighborhood to look for his parents or family."

Just then, a girl walked down the street and stopped near the nice lady. She said, "I can't find his family."

A minute later an older woman returned and also said: "I can't find his family."

The nice lady introduced the woman and girl to me.

"Look who we found! This is Mordechai, this little boy's brother!"

I took Naftali's hand and thanked the lady and her helpers for trying to reunite Naftali with his family. The lady smiled and said, "I'm happy to help. It's a mitzvah to return lost children to their families."

When I returned home, Ima said, "Thank you for taking care of Naftali."

"No, Ima, we must thank Hashem, Who takes care of little children, and the gemach for lost children," I replied, and then I told her the whole story.

CHAPTER THREE

A BREAD GEMACH

It was Friday afternoon. The house was clean. My older sisters were helping my little brothers and sisters bathe and get ready for Shabbos. Ima asked Efrayim, Eliezer and me to set the Shabbos table.

"You bring the cups and I'll bring the plates," Efrayim told me.

Suddenly we heard a knock. Eliezer ran to the door. Our neighbor, Chaya, was there.

"Can two Russian immigrants spend Shabbos with you?" she asked.

"We'll ask our Ima," Eliezer said.

"Ima!" Eliezer screamed, "Can we have Russians for Shabbos?"

"Of course," Ima replied.

"Of course," Abba also said.

"But Ima! We don't have enough food," Eliezer cried.

"We'll have enough, Eliezer," she said. She took some fish and chicken out of the freezer.

"But Russia is far away and it's almost Shabbos," Efrayim protested.

"They're not in Russia now. They're in America!" Abba replied.

Ima boiled some water and Abba brought in more chairs. But we children also wanted to help. We brought two more plates, two more cups, two more knives, two more forks and two more spoons to the table.

"Bring pretty napkins, in honor of the guests," Efrayim said.

Suddenly we heard another knock. Chaya was at the door again.

"Mrs. Cohen," Chaya asked, "can two more guests come?"

"Of course!" Ima replied. "I have plenty of fish and meat."

But when Ima closed the door, she remembered that she didn't have enough challah and it was almost Shabbos.

Ima called Chaya's mother and told her the problem. Chaya's mother said: "Don't worry. The Levi family has a bread and challah gemach."

Efrayim and I ran to the Levi's house. It was almost Shabbos. We knocked on the door and, when Mrs. Levi answered, we asked if she had some challah. "We have four extra guests for Shabbos!" we explained excitedly.

Mrs. Levi invited us into the kitchen. She opened her freezer and took out three challahs. She put them into the oven and warmed them up and then put them in a bag and gave it to us. We thanked her and ran home with the challahs.

We had a wonderful Shabbos. Our guests were very happy. We sang *zemiros* and told many stories. Abba explained the meaning of Shabbos to our guests. Of course, there was plenty of food and because of Mrs. Levi's bread and challah gemach there was even enough challah!

CHAPTER FOUR

A HOMEWORK GEMACH

We have a basement in our apartment building. It is very large and contains an old table, many old chairs, two wooden beds and some Sukkah boards.

On most days, no one enters it. Only during the summer—when my neighbor Chavi has a day camp there—is it used.

Then, when camp is over, my sisters Rina and Zisi help her clean the basement.

One winter day, Zisi said to Rina, "Let's go down to the basement."

"Why?" Rina asked.

"I want to look at it," she explained.

They opened the basement's creaky door and went inside. It was dark and cold. Rina turned on the light.

"I have an idea," Zisi said. "If we clean the chairs and tables, we can play here every day. We can even invite our friends. It'll be fun,"

"We can bring our younger brothers and sisters with us and let Ima rest in the afternoon. We can even do our homework here!" Rina suggested.

Zisi and Rina were very excited and made many plans.

At night, before they went to bed, Zisi said: "Let's make a gemach in the basement—a homework gemach. We'll invite all of the children in the neighborhood to do their homework in the basement. We can help the younger ones too!"

The next morning, they jumped out of bed. "Ima," they said. "We are opening a new gemach right here in our building."

"What kind of a gemach—a candy gemach?" she said laughing.

"No. A helpful gemach. A homework gemach!"

"That's a very good idea," she replied. "But our apartment is very small."

"That's no problem, Ima," Zisi said. "We'll have it in the basement. We'll help younger children do their homework. We can even bring toys for the babies."

"You are great kids," Ima said with a smile. Then she kissed them.

In the afternoon they made a big sign, and hung it up near the grocery store. It said:

> **HOMEWORK GEMACH**
>
> **Open every day from 4:30 p.m. to 6:30 p.m.**
>
> **1435 - 49th Street**

Children came to the homework gemach every day. My sisters helped them with their homework while their mothers rested. One day, a little girl named Sarah Schwartz showed them a note. It said:

Dear Mrs. Schwartz,

Sarah does her homework every day. She is doing very well in school.

Morah Roth

"Thank you so much for helping me!" Sarah told them. "My mother is so happy now!"

They were also happy, because it is a mitzvah to help others. And so they continue to help kids with their homework to this day!

CHAPTER FIVE

A BOTTLE GEMACH

My baby sister, Penina, loses her bottle at least five times a day. Sometimes three-year-old Miri takes the bottle and drinks from it herself. Sometimes Penina hides it and forgets where she put it.

Penina can't fall asleep without her bottle. If Ima can't find it, she asks us to look for it. We usually find it.

But one time we couldn't find the bottle.

My mother had put Penina to bed at seven o'clock. Rina and I were doing our homework.

Ima said: "The baby is quiet. I am going to visit Mrs. Katz—she is sick."

Soon after she left, Penina suddenly began to cry and soon her cries turned into screams.

"Give her a bottle," I said.

"Where is it?" Rina asked.

It wasn't on the table. It wasn't on the bed. It wasn't in the closet.

"B-a-t-i!" Penina cried.

"Penina, where is your bottle?" Rina asked.

"B-a-t-i," she cried again.

"Let's look in the kitchen," Rina suggested.

We searched the kitchen, the living room, and the porch, but couldn't find

friends! We live near the hall. When it snows or rains, we come here to dance with the bride and make her happy. We are a simcha gemach!"

My whole family smiled at the idea. We were happy someone could make my sister's wedding happier.

CHAPTER SEVEN

A CHICKPEA GEMACH

Early Friday morning the telephone rang. My older sister Zisi answered.

"Really? I don't believe it? That's so exciting! Mazal Tov!" she screamed.

"Who's on the phone? Who's on the phone?" we all asked screaming. We knew that something had happened, something good. But what? We jumped up and down screaming: "Tell us! Tell us who's on the phone!"

I wanted to ask Abba and Ima what had happened. I knocked on their door, but no one answered.

"Where is Ima? Where is Abba?" I asked.

"Do you want to speak with Mordechai?" I heard Zisi ask over the phone. Then she told me to come to the telephone.

"Abba is on the phone," Zisi said.

I went to the phone, and said, "Hello, Abba. Why aren't you at home? Where are you?"

"I'm in the hospital. Ima had a baby boy! You have a new brother."

We all began to sing and dance. I was the happiest of all because now there finally would be as many boys as girls in my family!

Later that day, when we returned from

school, Abba was home. He was in the kitchen. He said: "Everything is ready for Shabbos. But, we don't have chickpeas for the *Shalom Zachor*. What will we do?"

I was sad. Everyone I knew always had chickpeas at a *Shalom Zachor*.

Suddenly, I remembered Yitzchak Zilber from my class. His mother has an *arbess* gemach. She makes a lot of chickpeas once a month and puts them in the freezer. When someone needs them for a *Shalom Zachor,* she gives them to him.

It was nearly one o'clock. Yitzchak Zilber lives on 60th street, which is far from my house. But we needed chickpeas!

I ran all the way to Yitzchak's house and even ran up the steep flight of steps leading to his house. Yitzchak opened the door. He was surprised to see me.

"Yitzchak," I said, "Can you give me some chickpeas?"

He laughed. He thought that I wanted a snack.

"Yitzchak," I said, "My mother had a baby boy this morning! Now I have another brother!"

"Mazal Tov! Mazal Tov!" he cried, a big smile on his face.

Yitzchak called his mother. She was in the kitchen.

"Mordechai's mother had a baby boy!" he said.

"Mazal Tov! Mazal Tov," she cried.

"He needs chickpeas—lots of them."

Yitzchak's mother went to the freezer, and took out a large bag. "This has two pounds of chickpeas," she said. "Is it too heavy?"

"No," I replied. "Thank you very much. Abba will be very happy."

That night, after they finished eating their Shabbos meal, all our neighbors came to our *Shalom Zachor*.

"The chickpeas are delicious," everyone said.

"They have a special flavor," my father said. "The flavor of *chessed*!"

CHAPTER EIGHT

A SHABBOS GEMACH

It was Shabbos. Eliezer's seat was empty. So was Abba's. I made *kiddush.* Ima told us stories.

Where was Eliezer? Where was Abba? They were in the hospital. Eliezer did not feel well.

"What will Abba eat in the hospital?

Where will he sleep?" Efrayim asked.

"Does he have wine for *kiddush?* Does he have challah? Will he sing *zemiros* by himself? Is there a shul in the hospital?" Rina wondered.

Abba and Eliezer returned home after Shabbos. Abba said: "Eliezer feels better. His stomach doesn't hurt any more. He can even go to school tomorrow."

"What was wrong with him?" Ima asked. "Did he have appendicitis?"

"No," Abba said. "Eliezer, tell Ima what happened."

Eliezer began his long story:

"When we got to the hospital, the doctor asked me what hurt. I pointed to my stomach. The doctor examined me and gave me some medicine. I fell asleep. When I woke up, I felt better. It was already Shabbos and I wanted to go home."

But the doctor said, "I must check you again."

Then he asked: "Did you eat too much ice-cream?"

"I didn't eat ice cream," I explained. "I ate green apples."

"How many did you eat?" he asked.

"My friend Menachem and I wanted to see who could eat more green apples. Menachem ate only four. I won. I ate six."

The doctor laughed. Then he said, "You aren't sick. I have to send you home."

Abba was worried. It was already Shabbos and our house was far away from the hospital.

Suddenly, a man with a beard came over to him and said: "My name is Tuvia. Please come to our house for Shabbos. We live near the hospital. Every Shabbos I come to the hospital to see if people need a place to stay. We have a special room in our house for guests. We have a Shabbos gemach."

We said good-bye to the doctors and the nurses. The doctor smiled at me and said: "Next time don't eat so many green apples! Have a good Shabbos!"

We went home with Tuvia. His children met him at the door.

"Abba did you bring us a guest for Shabbos?" they asked.

"Two," he replied. "Show them the gemach room. They will sleep there, of course. Bring them some cake and tea. But don't give Eliezer any green apples!" he said with a big smile.

Tuvia's wife had already lit the candles, so we went to shul. Shabbos in their house was so much fun! We sang *zemiros,* told stories, studied the *parasha,* and ate really delicious food. On Motzai Shabbos Tuvia even gave us money for a taxi. And here we are!

Everyone laughed. Ima told Eliezer that he could have a banana, but no more green apples!

Abba then said: "Tuvia's house is like the tent of Avraham Avinu; guests are always welcome."

CHAPTER NINE

A GLASSES GEMACH

My brother Efrayim wears very thick glasses. Without his glasses, he can't see the blackboard, he can't see the Rebbe's face, and he can't even see how many olives are in his sandwich.

Everyone loves Efrayim because he is so kind and friendly. He is a good student, too. When his friends call him "Efrayim-*mishkafayim*," he doesn't get angry because he knows that they are joking. He laughs, too!

One day, Efrayim-*mishkafayim* ran into his class. He was very excited because there was a chumash test and he loves chumash. He even loves tests. He loves school. He loves everyone!

Just then, Asher ran out of the classroom and boom—Asher and Efrayim ran right into each other. Efrayim's glasses fell down and broke. There was a cut on Asher's face. The Rebbe washed Asher's face and told both boys to sit down. "You can take the test tomorrow, Efrayim. Your mother will get you new glasses this afternoon."

"But I love chumash and I want to learn today!" Efrayim cried. "I want my glasses now!"

Suddenly, Menachem had an idea. He said, "My neighbor, Mr. Weiner, has a glasses gemach. He lives one block away from school. His wife is at home. Perhaps he has glasses for Efrayim. Can I take Efrayim to the gemach now?"

"Yes," the Rebbe said. "What a great idea, Menachem!"

Menachem took Efrayim's hand and led him to the gemach.

Mrs. Weiner was home. She had Efrayim try on a bunch of glasses. Then she gave Efrayim a pair of glasses and said: "Return them when your mother buys you new ones."

The glasses looked very funny. They were very big and had black frames. They slipped down Efrayim's nose. He laughed and his friends laughed. Even the Rebbe laughed.

Efrayim was very happy. "Now I can see the blackboard. Now I can see the Rebbe. Now I can read the precious words of the chumash," he said.

CHAPTER TEN

A FAMILY GEMACH

Miri stood near Ima and cried, "Ima, bring me my doll."

"I'm busy now," Ima said. "Ask Zisi to bring you the doll."

"Zisi's busy too. She's doing her homework."

"Ask Rina!"

"I already asked her! She's talking on the telephone. She said, 'Not now.' "

"Ask Mordechai."

Miri went to the porch. I was there. I was talking to my best friend Shmuel.

"Look at that new building," Shmuel said. "No one lives there yet."

"It has four floors and a lot of apartments. I hope that a lot of kids will move in," I replied.

"Mordechai, please bring me my doll. It's on the top shelf," Miri cried.

"When new people move in, we'll help the little kids with their homework," I continued, ignoring Miri.

"I'll walk the little ones to school in the morning," Shmuel added.

"Mordechai, I want my doll. P-l-e-a-s-e."

"I'll help them shop and I'll ask Ima to bake them cakes for Shabbos."

Miri began to cry.

"Why is your sister crying?" Shmuel asked.

"She always cries," I replied, looking at Miri and shaking my head. "Let's go inside. I don't like crying!"

Suddenly, Ima came out to the porch. "Miri, why are you crying?" she asked.

"I want my doll. It's on the top shelf."

"Mordechai why didn't you give her the doll?"

"She didn't ask me for it."

"That's not true," Shmuel said. "She asked you for the doll. You just didn't hear her."

Ima went with Miri to the children's room and took down the doll.

"Here, Miri. Sit down and play," she said.

Miri stopped crying.

Shmuel and I came into the room. Suddenly, Shmuel said: "You know my little brother Avraham Yosef? Today, he wanted to come with me to your house. I told him: 'You can't come. I don't need a shadow.' Now I'm sorry. When I saw Miri crying, I remembered my brother. I'm sorry that I was mean to him. I think that we should help our own families, *not* only people in new buildings."

"Let's open a gemach," I happily said. "We will call it a family gemach. We will help all our brothers, sisters and parents."

"That's a great idea!" Shmuel said. "I'll open the gemach in my house. You can open one in your house. Everyone in the world can open this kind of gemach."

"Let's put a sign up which says: *A Gemach In Every House!*"

What a smart idea! The rules of the gemach will be: When Ima calls, come immediately. When little sisters cry, ask them what they want. Don't fight. Help your brothers and sisters with their homework," I said.

"Let's ask the newspapers to announce: There is a new gemach in town—a family gemach. Hours: all day, all night. Place: everywhere!" Shmuel added.